MW00907411

Nurses Are Superheroes Too

For more information regarding permissions or orders,
please email cssy_mitchell@yahoo.com

Cover Design and Illustration by: Danilo Cerovic

Hardcover ISBN: 978-1-7353426-0-3
Paperback ISBN: 978-1-7353426-2-7
Ebook ISBN:978-1-7353426-1-0

Library of Congress Control Number: 2020942117
Published by LadyBug Love2Read Publishing

To all my fellow nurses,
Thank You for all that you do.
Continue to save lives.

NURSES ARE SUPERHEROES TOO

Heroes Wear Scrubs and Stethoscopes

By C. P. Mitchell

Illustration by Danilo Cerovic

Hi, my name is Molly.
I am a nurse that takes care of really sick patients of all ages. It is really busy where I work, and I have to think fast on my feet! I keep an eye on lots of machines and tubes that record the patients' breathing and heart rates. I will be there in a flash to respond to problems to make sure that my patient receives the best care.

I am saving lives.

I am a Critical Care Nurse.

Hi, my name is Logan.

I am a nurse that helps deliver babies. I will never get tired of seeing the joy on the mom and dad's face when they hold their new baby for the first time. I am ready, any time – day or night – to provide care and support before, during, and after the delivery of the baby to make sure everyone is safe and healthy.

I am saving lives.

I am a Labor and Delivery Nurse.

Hi, my name is Poppy.

I am a nurse that takes care of babies, children, and teenagers. I give medicine to stop them from getting sick at school. I love working with my patients because of all the giggles we share, smiles I receive, and hugs I am given. I team up with mom and dad to keep track of their child's growth, making sure my patient receives the best care.

I am saving lives.

I am a School Nurse.

Hi, my name is Phoebe.

I am a nurse that takes care of patients before, during, and after surgery. In my job, teamwork really DOES make the dream work! I answer patients' questions and make sure they are healthy enough for the surgery. It's my responsibility to check the operating room is clean and has the right machines and instruments. After surgery, I stay with the patient until they wake up and are ready to go home.

I am saving lives.

I am an OR Nurse.

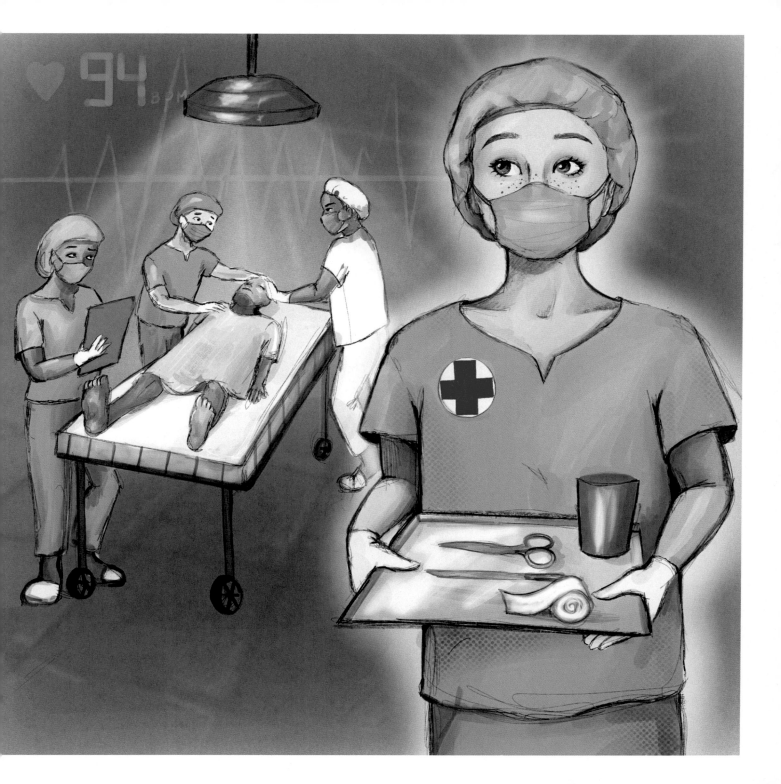

Hi, my name is Lucas.

I am a nurse that takes care of grown-ups that are sick or have had surgery. My job can change from one day to the next, so I have to stay on my toes! I give medicines and apply bandages when the patient is hurt. The beeping of the machines is music to my ears! Some days, I even get to teach patients and their families how to stay safe and healthy.

I am saving lives.

I am a Med-Surg Nurse.

Hi, my name is Harper.
I am a nurse that will stop the spread of bad bugs that make people sick. I know everything about the bad bugs, both big and small, AND I know how to treat them. I make sure nurses, doctors, family, and friends put on the right protective clothes, gloves, or masks before going into a patient's room. With my detective skills I am ready to fight off bad bugs.

I am saving lives.

I am an Infection Control Nurse.

Hi, my name is Nova.

I am a nurse that organizes care for a patient before they leave the hospital. I really enjoy talking, meeting, and helping people. It's fun to use my creative thinking to solve problems and to make sure I have the right care plan for each person. I work hard to make sure I've made the best plan for the patient to stay safe and healthy when they leave.

I am saving lives.

I am a Case Manager Nurse.

Hi, my name is Ayden.

I am a nurse that makes sure the hospital is safe for everyone who works there. When I see that one of the workers is in danger, it is my job to step in and make sure they don't get hurt. I train people how to lift or move heavy things without hurting their back, or how to use instruments safely. I detect danger and stop bad things from happening.

I am saving lives.

I am an Occupational Health Nurse.

Hi, my name is Gavin.

I am a nurse that teaches new nurses. I love to inspire others. Teaching is so much fun and brings me lots of joy. I educate nurses on the newest and best ways to treat patients. I change the future by sharing my knowledge and skills with new nurses to make sure that patients receive the best care.

I am saving lives.

I am a Nurse Educator.

Hi, my name is Jada.

I am a nurse that takes care of people with mental health issues. I am patient and always ready to listen and offer advice. I guide patients on how to think, feel, and act in a healthy way. With the right therapy and support I make sure my patient receives the best care.

I am saving lives.

I am a Mental Health Nurse.

Hi, my name is Eric.
I am the nurse who is responsible for everyone on the unit. I provide direction and guidance to the nurses and other workers. I monitor patient care to make sure they being well looked after. I am ready to step up and call the shots to help in an emergency.

I am saving lives.

I am a **Nurse Manager.**

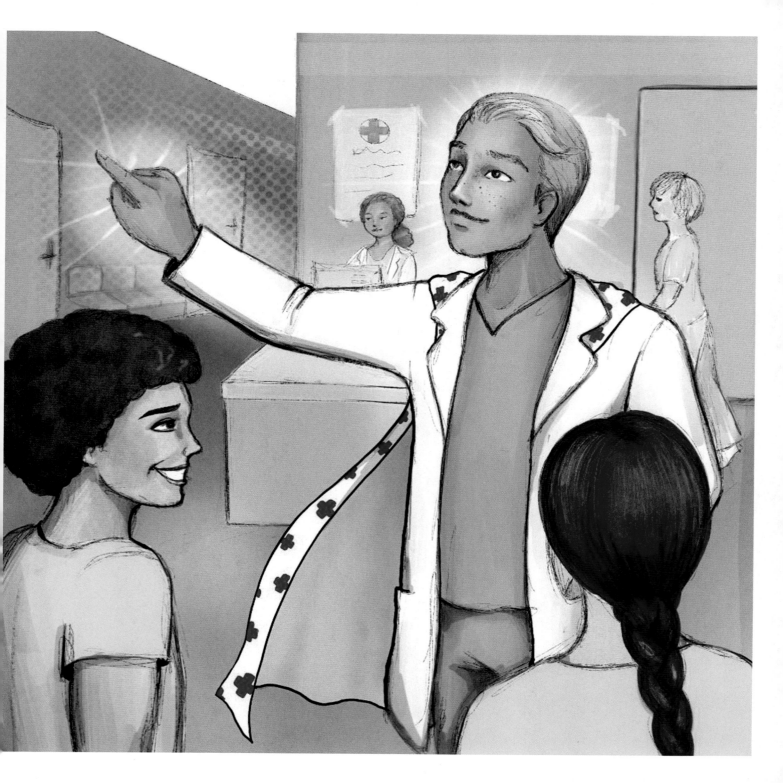

Hi, my name is Imani.
I am the nurse who looks after the whole nursing department in a hospital. I decide what is right and how to get a job done, but I also speak up for all nurses. I will lead and guide them as we work together to represent the mission of the hospital.

I am saving lives.

I am Chief Nurse Officer (CNO).

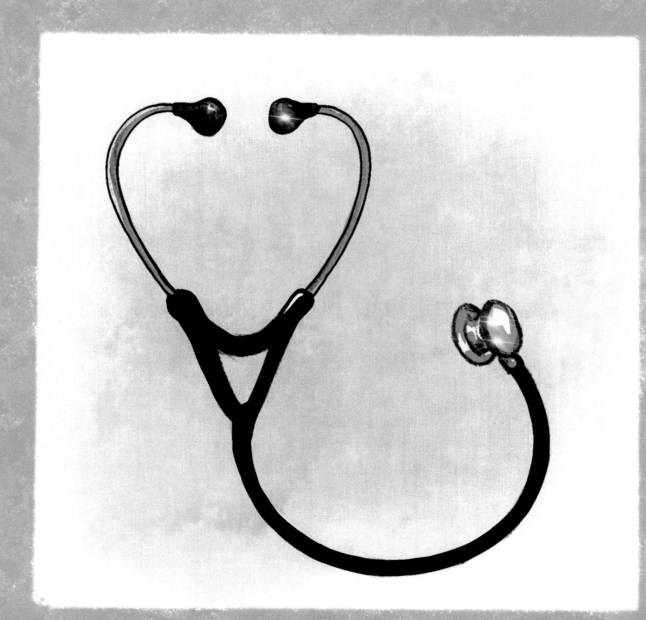

C. P. Mitchell is the fourth oldest out of her six siblings. She grew up in Long Beach, California, and is a proud aunt to five nieces and five nephews that bring her great joy every day. She still gets a good giggle when watching The Flintstones and enjoys watching Charlie Brown during the holidays. Becoming a nurse has been one of her biggest accomplishments in life. She is currently a Registered Nurse and is so proud to be achieving the dream she's had since she was six years old.

Danilo Cerovic is born in small town Prokuplje in Serbia. He started drawing when he was just 2 years old and he never stopped. Now he is a fashion/costume designer and freelance illustrator.

Made in the USA
Columbia, SC
26 August 2021